REED HOUSTON

authorHOUSE®

AuthorHouse™
1663 Liberty Drive
Bloomington, IN 47403
www.authorhouse.com
Phone: 1 (800) 839-8640

Published by AuthorHouse 07/24/2017

ISBN: 978-1-5462-0124-3 (sc)
ISBN: 978-1-5462-0122-9 (hc)
ISBN: 978-1-5462-0123-6 (e)

Library of Congress Control Number: 2017911393

Print information available on the last page.

Dedications

This book is dedicated to Peaches
I miss you more than words can express.

I would also like to thank everyone that supported
me with this project, I really appreciate You.

And a special thanks to all of the models that
brought my words to life through the use of their
imagery.

Dear You,

I think about you probably more than I should. My mind fills with "what could be's" and thousands of other possibilities. I often wonder if your mind finds me as well, I guess time will tell...or it won't. Either way you have filled my thoughts today. So when it gets quiet, just know I was thinking of you.

Me

Dear You,

Tonight...

I find myself lost in thought...

...thoughts of you
...me
...possibilities

Eyes closed...entering a meditative state as these words flow through me appearing on the screen...

Magically something comes from nothing and nothing becomes everything and I am will to do anything...

...just to see you again.

Me

Dear You,

There is a part me that is craving you though we have not met. Similar to a primal urge but deeper. I have to find you so this hunger can be satisfied... this thirst fulfilled...this Love created.

Me

Dear You,

I want to be intimate with you in such a way that no words are spoken…only energy is felt…skin against skin…soul against soul…you against me… intimately.

Me

Dear You,

Imagining that first kiss...that first time I miss...
you...that intimate touch...that just enough not too
much...the foreplay...the afterplay...the way...you
come when I call you...the way...we...just...be.

Me

Dear You,

Loving you would be a beautiful wreck, yet I crave the collision...you could be the best worst decision I ever made...like walking barefoot on a sharp blade...you are like gravity and I am free falling... plummeting into your love and pain...

Me

Dear You,

I exhale just to inhale you...my air...my breath...I dig your depth...with every inch of my soul...the uncontrollable urge to touch your spirit overwhelms me...aroused by your femininity...lured by your sexuality...frozen by the beauty of your reflection... sublime erections resulting from your sweet lyrics of love and lust...it is a must that I experience every ounce of you...you are my high...I am in desperate need of a fix...simply put...y o u a r o u s e m e...the touching of our souls spells bliss like locked angels twisted in flight...delightfully tilted in the skewness of you...bathing in the newness of you...wanting to write my name upon your nudity...craving this spiritual unity...breathing you in deeply...

Me

Dear You,

Keeping me awake in the stillness of night
Even when I should know better
Nothing compares to getting lost in thoughts
of you…
You have entered my spirit
And, I welcome you to remain...

Me

Dear You,

Yet another sleepless night as I desperately try to cope with the absence of your warmth in my bed. I miss your touch. I miss the way our bodies just "fit" together as we slumber.

I miss you.

Me

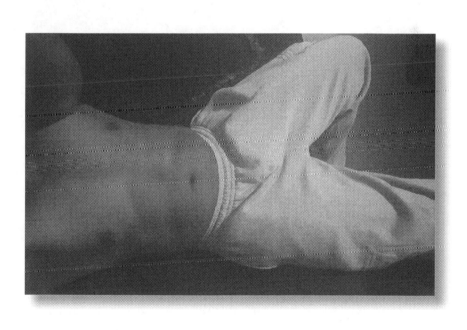

Dear You,

There was a moment in time when all I breathed
was you
When the pain came...all I needed was you
Times changed, the rains came and you forgot
my name
No calls, no texts, of course no more sex
Not even a fuck you
It was then in that moment I realized my value
The world seemed colder and I grew older
Refusing to trust only offering lust
Just a bunch of meaningless actions
Temporary satisfactions
I fucked twelve chicks all in the name of you
In search of what I lost
Not really knowing what to do
I hated what I'd become
It was too late...the damage was done
Life was no longer fun
It was a game I played
Innocents got slayed

Then one day it all changed
I could barely remember your name
I erased all of your pain
My thoughts were clear
My life was new
Most important...I couldn't remember you
My genesis was about to begin
And finally...finally...I could breathe again

Me

Dear You,

Today...I thought about you in the most intense way...thought about all the things I wanted to say...staring at the world below from my window seat...just thinking...thinking about a future with you...thinking about the things I want to do...the moments I want to share...the memories I want to create...how I want to direct fate...and how I don't want to wait...I need the shine of your sun in my life...too soon to talk about wife...but I can see that too...I'm just a better me when I'm connected to you...so today...I just wanted you to know...I'm thinking about you in the most intense way.

Me

Dear You,

No you didn't cheat on me
No you didn't get pregnant
No you didn't try to destroy me
But... You did hurt me

You did take me for granted
You did treat me less that I deserve...
But... I allowed it

Not because I didn't love me, but because I loved
you I trusted you like no other I felt safe...
I never thought I would have to say, "What you did
was fucked up" I just thought that you knew me
well enough to know what would hurt me before
you did it

Even after the fact, I shouldn't have to say, "Hey,
I'm hurting"
To get you to think about my feelings
The truth is...
You hurt me...

You hurt me...
YOU HURT ME...

Not my ex...not some chick down the street...
You...my most trusted friend...
YOU

Behind all of the excuses
Behind all of the reasons
Behind all of the issues

You hurt Me

You may never want to face it
You may never acknowledge my feelings
You may never think I'm worth bending for
You may never see me for the person I am
You may never appreciate me for the friend that
I was
You may never respect me for the man that I am
You may never recognize the damage you did
You may never get it
But in the end...You hurt Me

Dear You,

Tonight I miss you as I lay on the couch beneath the cool breeze of my oscillating fan...drifting off when I remember our moments of passion and my body awakens so here I find myself texting out my emotions wondering if I will ever share them with you...I know I'm free to think of you even though the thought of how I could be with you makes me feel so vulnerable yet comforting... I live in this conflict with you somewhere between forward and backwards between here and there...I lay my head on this pillow and just imagine it's you that I'm close too...

Me

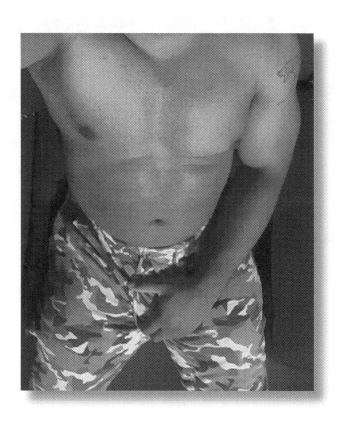

Dear You,

I want to sleep with you snuggled on the couch,
your legs wrapped around mine. Our breathing
synchronized as we slumber.

Me

Dear You,

You will find me betwixt lyrics of unfinished songs...somewhere between forgotten sunsets and the memorable dawn...between the sound of raindrops and rays of light...between thought and memory...between laughter and tears...between comfort and fear.

Between here and there, between now and then... that's where you find...

Me

Dear You,

I dreamed...
   I hoped....
      I wished...
           We met...
           We created...
           We loved...
                  You left...
                  I hurt.

                  Me

Dear You,

Mistake after mistake I make while I try to
wait for you...I know you will understand me
completely...so I search endlessly...taking chances I
wouldn't normally take all in the name of love and
connection hoping it will point me in the direction
of you...any clue...any sign...something that leads me
to your divine...your sacred...you...I crave you more
than you know...and desperately hope I find you...in
this lifetime.

Me

Dear You,

I miss your body heat. I miss the love we made between the sheets...on the floor...against the door... room to room. I am imagining the feel of your skin against mine, your lips against mine. I remember your kiss...I remember all of the things I miss.

Me

Dear You,

Once upon a time I knew you...

...your highs and lows...the curve of your smile...the whisper of your voice...the echo of your orgasms...

I knew you...

>...inside and out...I shared your pain...dared your dreams...danced with your spirit...laid in your warmth...hid in your lap...

I knew you...but now...I don't.

Me

Dear You,

What we had no longer exists and normally I would
be pissed but instead I find myself thinking of
butterflies...rainy days...wise words my grandmother
would say...and just like you these are beautiful
too but most of all by me missed...I will always
remember that cold week in November...when our
souls mated before we ever dated...and how bright
our fire burned before it suddenly faded...

Me

Dear You,

Thinking about the last time love was made...

Me

Dear You,

My love was meant to be given away and since I currently have no one to give my love to, I have decided to share my heart with you. My joys...my pains...my hopes...my sorrows...my dreams of new tomorrows...I give to You, Me...completely.

And, although I do not know you...I can honestly say I Love You.

Me

Dear You,

Like fire and flame we will burn brighter than any star in any midnight sky in any universe...our heat will scorch the earth setting everything ablaze...both reality and fantasy will be touched by our Love...

Me

Dear You,

I'm just sitting here...waiting...waiting to love you...
but not just any regular type love...I'm talking that
deep shit...that without you my heart doesn't beat
shit...that illogical shit...mythological shit...the defy
a god just to eat your forbidden fruit shit...that cock
back the nines for you I'll shoot shit...that forever
and a day, fuck what other people say shit...that I
would cry for you...die for you...tell all kinda lies
for you...feel for you...steal for you...who the fuck I
gotta kill for you...always keep it real for you...but
for now...I'm just sitting here...waiting...waiting to
love you...

Me

Dear You,

I would have loved you until the end of time and still remained for the rebirth...beyond heaven and earth even through the gates of hell...I would have loved you...but you chose another and I watched as he smothered your flame...it's a shame to see a beautiful songbird caged with no melody to sing... yet I respected your choice to surrender your voice...well maybe to some degree as I wonder how differently things would have been if you were loved by me...but I realized some chains can't be broken especially when bondage is chosen...

Me

Dear You,

Truth is...

You cross my mind a lot and the harder I try to move on, the more I find myself thinking of you.

Me

Dear You,

I thought this was supposed to get easier with time but somehow you keep creeping into my mind...it starts as a whisper...your name...your face...then my thoughts are all over the place...remembering you... imagining you...missing you...craving you...yet there is nothing I can do...nothing that will bring you back to me...so I am stuck in this misery until Time decides to set me free...

Me

Dear You,

We made our music but our song came to an end...
yet the melody still plays clearly in my head...
reminding me of a rhythm I once called ours.

Me

Dear You,

You have been on my mind a lot lately. So much I have felt the need to express to you. If you ever get serious about love, let me know. Because if you ever allow me to love you, I will never stop.

Me

Dear You,

I miss you more than I ever thought I would...it hurts to not be able to see you again...to touch you... to hold you...everything is such a mess now...I can't call...I can't text....I have lost all connection with you and I hate it...I hate losing you...I hate never getting the chance to love you and no matter how much people tell me it's probably for the better...this doesn't feel better...it feels horrible...I hate missing you like this.

Me

Dear You,

I am ready for something real...I don't care how it exists or what label it carries as long as it is tangible enough for me to believe in it...depend on it...trust in it...evolve in it...I am ready to pour energy into something that is greater than myself...

Me

Dear You,

I want to wipe away your tears...hear your laughter
in my ears...protect you from your fears...so I am
reaching out...I hear your silence and I respect your
absence...yet that does not stop me from missing
your presence.

Me

Dear You,

We don't have to agree
I don't have to be right
Just existing in your world and loving you is more
than enough
Holding hands while we share our lives walking
through time
I will protect and defend you
I will love and care for you
You will be safe with me...

Me

Dear You,

I need to make love to a woman and not just in the physical sense...I mean to arouse her spirit...comfort her soul...wipe her tears...remove her doubts and fears...protect her heart...let her know she is a part of something greater...I need her to feel me, not just in her body but in her heart and mind...I want to take the love within me and pour it over her...saturate her...reassure her...support her...hold her...love her...I really need to make love to a woman in ways that only a man like me can...

Me

Dear You,

I want to make love to you...not just your body...your mind...your heart...and if you allow...your soul...

I have loved you for awhile and just didn't know how to express it. Yes, I Love You. I knew it when things started changing but I denied it until I found myself missing you just as I am now. I wake up with you on my mind daily. Hoping to hear from you... hoping to see you again...hoping to kiss you again... hoping to hold you...hoping that I connect with you beyond the physical. You already know the pleasures of my sexual love...now it's time you experience the beauty of my romantic love...my protective love...my healing love...my love love...I know "love" is a word that scares people. Even as expressive and fearless as I am...I hesitated. But no more... I Love You...

You don't have to feel the same...you don't have to avoid me...just letting you know where I am.

Me

Dear You,

When I realized that I missed you and you didn't care it opened my eyes to what was inside me...I loved you and I hated myself for it...I wished the pain would end but instead it taunted me out of my sleep and found myself drowning in tequila just to stop thinking about you and the memories we created that were brought to a halt by a few simple words that carried way too much weight...and in that moment the years of passion that we once shared...evaporated...

Me

Dear You,

I love you yet our lips have never touched...I imagine it would be the sweetest kiss I've ever known...you control my laughter...transforms my energy...you brings out the best in me...you are the pleasure I have yet to experience...You are Love.

Me

Dear You,

Tonight is one of those nights that I could have
made love to you all night...slow stroking against
the sound of distant thunder and falling raindrops...
our love song sung acapella...our bodies in sync...
passions explored...energies released...

Me

Dear You,

Once upon a time we used to fuck each other's brains out...then I watched teary-eyed as the Love slowly drained out...No matter how hard I try can't get the stains out...No choice but to try and wait this pain out...

I remember wrinkled sheets and twisted pillow cases...lovemaking echoes and pleasure faces...I remember the vibration of my name across your tongue...but now that's long gone...too much damage was done and now we can't go on...

Sometimes I wish we could return to that place...I miss touching your face...but that's just my overactive mind...as I still remember what happened last time...

Me

Dear You,

Without You I am slowly dying so there is no need in lying as if I don't need You…as if I don't breathe You…my heart beats You…You…the One that stays on my mind, that causes me to lose track of time…the One that lives between these lines… the One mere words cannot simply define…yea You…I get lost in Your eyes…Your smile…Your mannerisms…the way You twirl Your locks when You have naughty thoughts…the way You move… the way You sooth…Me…amuse me with the sway of Your hips…the way You bite Your lips…I sip from You greedily…You are my Fire…my Water…my Air… my Earth…You give birth to my consciousness…and I am bound to Your existence…and in this moment I miss You…

Me

Dear You,

I would have loved you with all that I had but at the time you couldn't see me...I wasn't the tallest...the richest...the most attractive...but I might have been the most kind...most thoughtful...most loving...but I understand...it's hard to see the inside of a man if the outside is what sets off the spark...I knew you were a shot in the dark anyway...it was hard to sit back and look as with each love you got took... used...abused...emptied...and discarded...I tried my hardest not to interfere...but it was just too difficult to just sit there quietly while the beauty of you was dying silently...I would have loved you if you would have given me the chance...now so much has happened and we can't go back...just wish things were different...really...I do.

Me

Dear You,

She is beautiful to me...the sound of her voice
calms my inner storms...she bring a light to my
life that few ever see...she makes my complex
simple...she actually gets me...the real me...the
naked me...straight...no chaser...no facade...no
smoke...no mirrors...I only wish we were nearer in
this lifetime because I honestly don't want to wait
another...

Sometimes in this sea of confusion I wonder if
I am secretly waiting on her to free herself so
that we can connect finally...am I subconsciously
comparing and disqualifying because they don't
touch me like she does...her laughter is contagious,
my soul dances...entranced by the melody...like an
enchantress she transforms my tears into liquid
sunshine...even across distant phone lines...I am
bound to her and she to me...

My only wish is that universe sees fits for us to occupy the same place at the same time in this existence...

If only...

Me

Dear You,

I wanted to connect with you deeply but you were
not ready to receive me completely...rejection in any
form is not something I accept easily...so I sought
out another to please me...so here I am deeply
thrusting another while deep inside I would rather
be your lover but apparently...that wasn't meant
to be otherwise it would you and I locked in this
naked embrace...but instead...here I am kissing a
different face...

Timing is everything so maybe at different time and
different place we can be in the same place at the
same time...

Me

Dear You,

The reflection of me was seen in you as I bare my all before the queen in you unclothed...naked...I bow before you simply to adore you...to lay within your pleasure...satisfy...intensify beyond measure... to dance with you against music self-created... spiritually mated...locked like twisted fingers... forever connected...my nakedness reflected...in the eyes of you.

Me

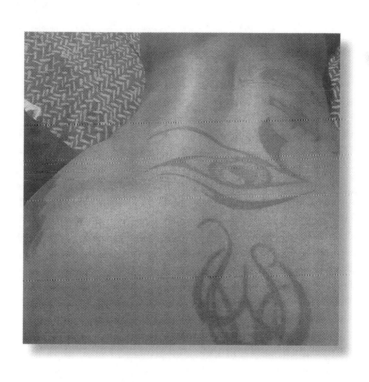

Dear You...

Slow tunes of eroticism echo against my bedroom
walls throughout the night into the early morning...

I close my eyes and imagine You beneath me...
inviting me to please You...stroking You slowly
to lyrics mixed with sex and love...your fingertips
against my skin pulling me deeper inside You...I
bathe in each moan and each sigh...losing myself in
your pleasure...

If only You were here...

Me

Dear You,

I felt a comfort in you like no other
But you chose to give your love to another
A special part of me died that day
When there were no more words to say
I cursed your name
You became the blame for all my pain
The weight of the world crushed me
I no longer had trust in me
See…
Trusting me led me to you
I had no clue of the damage you would do

Me

Dear You,

As much as I hate missing You, I love having You to miss.

Me

Dear You,

You often stated to me that you were more than just your sex

But I noticed it was how you measured yourself

You pleasured yourself

By offering views and clues to your naked hips

Just a couple more clicks to the key that unlocked your punani

Or at least that's the deception you believed while deceiving yourself

I saw a beauty in you that you had yet to discover

Too interested in the insignificant words of others that only had their minds on the prize between your thighs to even lend credibility to words I spoke genuinely and freely

Somehow I became just another dick trying to paint your walls and you missed it all...my love...my devotion...my eternal pledge to you...I saw the beauty in you but you failed to see the beauty in me while subtly selling your sexuality for all eyes to see...

Me

Dear You,

I know you can hear me
I know you can feel me
I know you understand me
When I was lost in the seas of confusion and
uncertainty
You called my name
I heard you
I felt you
I understood you
It was the sweetest thing I've ever known
In that moment I knew where I belonged
I knew I had to know you and you already knew me
You saw me thru different eyes and helped me to see
what was hidden to me
You helped me find me

Me

Dear You,

You needed to be felt
I needed to be touched
You needed to say I love you
I needed to hear those words
You needed to cry
I needed to comfort

Me

Dear You,

I care about you

it's time to talk

it's time to be honest

even if the honest answer is...idk or idc or i'm scared

if you are falling for someone else then say that

whatever it is between us...good or bad it needs
to be discussed or that resentment will creep in...
simply not fucking me and avoiding the issues will
not keep this from happening...I need to know how
you really feel you need to know how I feel and we
need to try to come to some kind of agreement, or
understanding

we are in a relationship no matter how dysfunctional
and undefined...it is what it is...and its broken...

Me

Dear You,

The sun is setting yet I am still hopeful...
daydreaming at
night...thinking...wondering...imagining...releasing
my heart into the universe so that it may someday
return to me...in the form of You.

Me

Dear You,

I hope that as you are reading this, you know that I am ready to receive you unabbreviated. I want your good, your bad, your ugly to be a part of my life. I want to wake up each day to your bad habits and love you even more for being imperfect.

Me

Dear You,

Been thinking about you since we said our goodbyes...whatever I "thought" I felt just multiplied... "having" you just made me want you more as I remembered all the things I missed... your kiss...your touch...showers...holding you at night...and as all of this was taking place...I was just happy...and no matter how many times I told myself to just stay in the moment...I wanted "you" to be my life...I thought about the "would be's" and "should be's" during our hours of pleasure...all I know is...I can't get enough...after all this time...you STILL stay on my mind...and right as you are reading this just know that...I...want...you.

Me

Dear You,

I wanna remember forgotten mythologies and share philosophies with you. Ready for you to be my Genesis.

Me

Dear You,

I am looking forward to the creation of our memories. The millions of pixels that will capture our most intimate of moments. The replay as we share our stories of love, laughter, and loss. I cannot wait to be a part of the beautiful world that we create.

Me

Dear You,

I will know her...because she will see me...in a sea of unknown faces...she will find me...our spirits will mate before we ever touch...she will know me...

She will...

Me

Dear You,

All I need is one chance…one opportunity…one moment for just you and me…I have dreamed about this for a while now…forget all the why's and how's…I want you…and you know I feel it…I have imagined your kiss…your touch…your skin…I pictured us making love over and over again…by the candlelight…by the moonlight…all night… 'til daylight…position after position…I need to experience you in this lifetime…so if we are ever in the same place at the same time…I'm going for it… for that moment you will be mine…and I plan to enjoy you thoroughly…repeatedly…I just need one moment…one moment for just you and me.

Me

Dear You,

I fell first so I could be waiting for whenever you decided to let go and trust me to catch you...

Let go of...

Fear...
Pain...
Disappointment...
Lies...
Insecurities...

If you fall...I will catch you...

Me

Dear You,

I fought for you because I never wanted you to become a distant memory...a lover whose face I can barely remember...whose name only crosses my mind when that song once forgotten comes within my listening space...you were special and I wanted you to stay that way...but nevertheless...you are not here...and I let go...and now we will never know the beauty that would have been us...

Me

Dear You,

Anxiously awaiting your arrival so that my life as I know it can end...giving birth to new dimensions of existence with You.

This has become my constant daydream starring You.

Me

Dear You,

Forever and Never are two words I try to avoid the usage of...but I know you are gone forever and I will never hear from you again...it pains me greatly because see...I loved you...I love you...and I will love you long after you forget your memories of me... long after I become one of the names you can't remember...long after everything that once mattered no longer does...I never wanted to let you go... forever.

Me

Dear You,

The most beautiful poetry I have yet to write is waiting on you to enter into my life. My perfect muse...the one I will forever choose...beyond the realm of infinity...in this or any other alternative existence...our love shall be made eternal by the words I have yet to write...

...about You.

Me

Dear You,

You are still beautiful to me even though you are just a memory I revisit from time to time when thoughts of you cross my mind or I see a sign that reminds me of the time I once had with you...very few have had this effect on me but for some reason you do...my pride won't let me tell you that I think about you...but I do...

Me

Dear You,

At a different time and in a different place we were once lovers. So when I meet you again for the first time, it will be as glorious as the last time. Time...space...structure...conventional rules will become nothing but poorly defined words in some unknown dictionary. Nothing will make sense yet it will all make perfect sense in the same moment. We will be new familiar lovers and will mate in the oxymoronic greyness.

Me

Dear You,

Looking forward to sharing rainstorms with you. Perhaps we can make love to the beat of raindrops against our skin. Thoroughly enjoying each other beneath the cover of grey skies.

Me

Dear You,

Here I sit, impatiently waiting and wanting to fully enjoy the intimacy you will bring to my life that I so desperately crave. With each kiss, passion will be redefined. I will be elated to be yours and honored you are mine.

Me

Dear You,

"You" are my favorite position.

Me

Dear You,

I will know you when I find you because you will allow me to be free. Free when others tried to suffocate me. You will see the truth in my dualities and accept me. Instead of judgment, you will show empathy. That is how I will know you. Hopefully we will find each other soon.

Me

Dear You,

When you are ready for Love...I will be here waiting. All you have to do is find me. Nothing would give me greater joy than to be the reason for your smile.

Me

Dear You,

I desperately desire to create an infinity with you. Somewhere between never and forever...existence and oblivion...life and death...

On the edge of everything and nothing, we will create a spectrum of lifetimes in our infinitely defined moment.

Me

Dear You,

You dare me to revisit to words once written beneath past moons before the time you existed in my physical universe. My subconscious was always your playground as I awaited the awakening of your arrival. Skin against skin...flesh against flesh...this connection will manifest into the realm of reality.

Me

Dear You,

Last night through this morning, I had erotic yet sensual thoughts of you. They were so real I could feel the warmth of your body next to mine. The anticipation of your touch overloaded my senses each time I closed my eyes. I could feel your fingertips tiptoeing down the small of my back. I awaited the softness of your lips against my skin. Thoughts of you are the reason behind this early morning erection.

Me

Dear You,

When our paths finally cross, I want to make love so passionately that each thrust feels like a matter of life and death and each kiss holds the past, present, and future in one moment.

Me

Dear You,

I daydream about how deeply I want to fall and rise in love with you. I imagine us revolving around each other like twin stars in the cosmos. Heavenly bodies locked in total synchronicity...eternally. A mystery to all that gaze upon the beauty of us. I can see our love so clearly that I get lost in it frequently.

Today...I was thinking about You.

Me

Dear You,

When You arrive...be prepared. Be prepared to be loved like You have never been loved before. Brace yourself because the intensity alone is enough to frighten most. Just know You are safe with me and I will not take You anywhere I am not prepared to hold your hand through. I know this is a lot to take in...yet...my hand awaits yours.

Love,

Me

Dear You,

I don't wanna fight, tear You down, or break You...if You let me...I will restore, uplift, and love You...if... You...let...me...

Me

Dear You...

I just want to be the circumference around your center so that our boundaries become blended... so that your ending and my beginning cannot be determined.

Me

Dear You...

I want to dive so deeply into You that I lose myself
and discover myself simultaneously.

Me

Dear You...

I could get high off you...if I chose to...let you flow through my veins...let you ease my pains...I could be a slave to your voodoo...yea...I could really get high off you...

Me

Dear You...

I write about Love when I write about You.

Me

Dear You...

Gods will be defied and Deities cursed as I explore the depths of Love with You. We can created our own Universe, defining the cosmos as we choose... bending Reality with our Imagination.

Me

Dear You...

If I could kiss your skin daily...I would...here...
there...especially there...tracing each intricate line of
your feminine form...

If I could...

Me

Dear You...

I let go of everything I ever knew just so I could get to know you.

No regrets.

Me

Dear You...

Too often I find myself lost in thoughts of You.
Wondering where you are, what you are doing,
when we will meet. I like to imagine that you are
somewhere...wondering the same about me.

See you soon.

Me

Dear You...

I know you are afraid of heights and skydiving is not your thing. I know you are terrified about falling because up until now hitting the ground hurts like hell. But what if I told you that I have wings...And, if as long as you hold my hand, I will never let go. We can fly to heights unknown together and falling will become a distant memory...for both us.

Me

Dear You...

I am willing...
I am ready...
I am waiting...

Me

Dear You...

You are the words unspoken...the kiss un-stolen...
the "what if"...the untold story that lingers in my
mind...as I remember a time...not so long ago...
when we touched without touching... "regret" is not
the proper term...but I often find myself wondering
what might have been...

Me

Dear You...

I cannot wait to love you...

...verbally...lyrically...mentally...emotionally...
spiritually...completely...eternally...

Today, this is where I am...wish you were here.

Me

Dear You,

When you are ready for Love...I will be here waiting. All you have to do is find me. Nothing would give me greater joy than to be the reason for your smile.

Me

Dear You,

I loved you...you tolerated me. Unfortunately, it took me too long to see. Before I knew it, I lost all of me. While you sat there, nonchalantly, pretending not to see.

Mc

Dear You,

In my head, we were beautiful. I thought we would figure love out, go against the odds, find a way to make it work...

Now, all I can think about is how I wish things were different or that I was somewhere else...

Me

Dear You,

The words "I'm sorry" and "Thank you" carry a lot of weight to me. Unfortunately, their absence from your vocabulary was heavier.

Me

Dear You,

I was worth the fight but you never bothered to swing.

Me

Dear You,

365 days and now we part ways...too many words said and unsaid...we found each other once... hopefully the universe will see fit for us to find each other again...until then...remember us.

Me

Dear You,

I thought of a million things I wanted to say to you...then proceeded to hit backspace a million times.

Me

Dear You,

Our fire burned bright enough to light the outer atmosphere until all of the air disappeared as our love suffocated itself, tragic, suicidal yet necessary for evolution, the absence of resolution gave birth to a revolution that move us from together to apart...

Me

Dear You,

One of the saddest moments in my life was realizing there was nothing else to say but goodbye.

Me

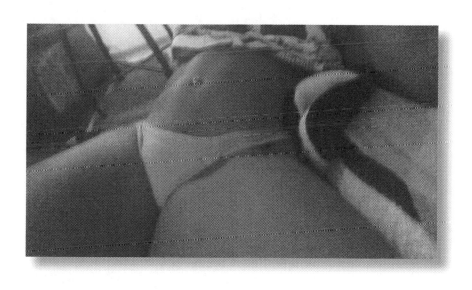

Dear You...

I really wanna stroke your clit with the tip of my fingers through your panties until...

Yea...

Passionately yours,

Me

Dear You,

Your faith in me inspires me to challenge myself.

Me

Dear You,

I am thoroughly and unequivocally convinced that if you were here this night would begin with your head in my lap and my fingers in yours.

Me

Dear You,

There are times I look into your eyes and I want to hit fast forward to better days then hit slow motion to enjoy every second thoroughly.

Me

Dear You,

I am finding myself falling even deeper in love with you. This is both exciting and scary to me at the same time.

Me

Dear You,

I need to do bad things to you. Whether behind closed doors or out in the open, naked or clothed just know it is my intent to use every ounce of my creativity on You.

Me

Dear You,

I have come to hate our good-bye's.

Me

Dear You,

I love you so much that being away from you creates a pain that only you can soothe.

Me

Dear You,

You are the porn that continuously replays in my mind.

Me

Dear You,

You are worth having difficult conversations with.

Me

Dear You,

I want to fall so deeply into You that the Universe I once knew ceases to exist.

Love,

Me

Dear You,

The music we make vibrates and resonates in frequencies yet to be known against my soul.

Me

Dear You,

I miss you a lot...more than I tell you although I mention it often. You are a constant thought, my favorite memory...

Me

Dear You,

When I see you again...

.....brace yourself.

Me

Dear You,

I wish missing you wasn't an option.

Me

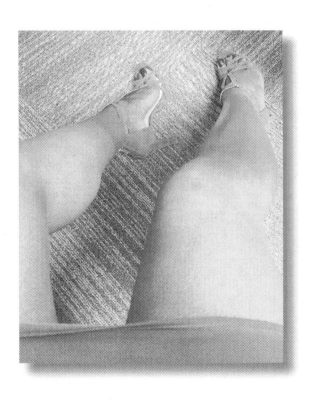

Dear You,

The majority of my life's moments are spent thinking about you.

Me

Dear You,

There are times I just wish You were here so we could have deep conversations without talking.

Me

Dear You,

I am thirsty...

          ...for You.

Me

Dear You,

Entering your universe has redefined my existence. Transforming me from mortal to…

Creator

Me

Dear You,

Beneath the light of the full moon and in the quietness of this night, my thoughts are on You... You are the clarity in my clouded mind and I pray that one day my words find...You.

Me

Dear You,

Somewhere near the intersection of Like and Love, I discovered...You are my Path.

Me

Dear You,

The more I discover about You...the more I learn about myself.

Me

Dear You,

The romantic in me was desperately screaming out to You, could you hear me? I could feel your energy as if it was memory, though I have yet to experience the pleasure of your touch...your kiss...so how can I miss that which I do not know? I do not know...but somehow this feeling exists...thereby You must too. I am here...waiting for You to appear.

Me

Dear You,

I craved You...long before we became intimate...the anticipation buried me beneath beautiful thoughts of You...naked...skin against my skin...me within... moving...out then in...losing myself between your lines...more accurately speaking...between your thighs...staring deep into your eyes...listening attentively for your escaping sighs...my fingers twisted in your hair...savoring each stroke...as if it were my last...

Me

Dear You,

I can't really find the words to describe what we were so I guess it was indescribable...

Yet in the midst of the undefined and uncategorized we found each other and the "undefinedness" was more than enough definition for us to become what we are...

Somewhere in the unknown...we knew each other... like past lovers...we are familiar...like the deep penetration of intelligent conversation craved by the sapiosexual...we are multisexual connecting on multiple levels...experiencing multiple pleasures... carving our time into existence...

Me

Dear you,

I see the love in your eyes...I know You hate good-bye's...I hope You see how hard I try not to make you cry...

I love how You and I became we...and yours and mine became ours...You asked for something sweet to wake up to...well see You in about two hours...

Me

Dear You

You provoke me to stroke you deeply until we both get sleepy…late nights, early mornings sex before dawn and we're both still yawning but the pleasure is immeasurable as we move from the bed to the dresser then the bathroom counter staring at the naked images in the mirror until what's blurry becomes clearer and I want you nearer until our beginnings and endings cannot be determined... until my length and your depth become so blended that our bodies transcend until we collapse in the ecstasy we created.

Me

Dear You,

I found the center of her universe and admired its beauty. My key fit perfectly, unlocking all of her secrets. Now I stand guard, protecting her with my existence.

Me

Dear You,

We lied to ourselves calling it fucking when all the while we were making love...the depth of our emotions remained unspoken while we found ourselves lost in the strokin'...somewhere between multiple orgasms and cuddling, the undefined became defined in our minds...

So somewhere in the midst of coming together we came together and it was all we needed.

Me

Dear You,

You deserve all of my nastiness.

Me

Dear you,

I know you are looking for me although we exist on different planes I feel your energy around me your face and your name I miss you more than you know I was not ready to let go.

Me

Dear You,

Beneath dreary skies I look into your weary
eyes and see forever...and whatever I was about
to say suddenly became so unimportant as I
found myself lost in thoughts about the future
we imagined together...instantly I feel high as I
reach for your hand and your fingers find mine...
locked...embraced...grey skies erased as you are my
sunshine...

Me

Dear You,

I surrender to the pleasure of being yours...

Me

Dear you,

We are a beautiful mix of love, sex, and friendship.

Me

Dear You,

I look into your eyes and can barely remember the time before I knew you.

Me

Dear You,

Yea...I think of You often...my imagination runs
wild...from ink on your naked skin...to the pleasure
of pain cold steel against bare wrists...our tongue
twist in the midst of our foreplay...my fingers
explore all of your secrets...your orgasms sing in my
ear...our bodies create melodies...neighbors hear
our vibrations...we introduce each other to raw
sensations...

I revisit this place...often.

Me

Dear You,

I'm nervous as fuck and you aren't the reassuring type...but too many times I have been lured by loved and then decapitated...even when I hesitated, they just waited for me to get comfortable before introducing me to the seduction of the katana...the blade was dull...they took their time...I can still feel my heart grind against the steel...cutting deeper into my soul...I know you don't understand...but even if you did, you aren't the reassuring type.

Me

Dear You,

Although I only knew You for a brief moment in time…the impact of our collision was very real… so real that when You decided to walk away it left a difficult void to fill…it feels like a crater resides where you used to be…desperately missing your energy…we were like twin flames dancing across time and space…You were what I needed when I needed it…

Fate crossed our paths…Destiny separated us…the course of my Life was changed…if only for a brief moment in time…

You will be missed…timelessly…

Me

Dear You,

So many unsaid things I wanted to say. Instead I chose silence and watched you walk away.

Me

Dear You,

Your touch brings me to the center of my chaos. You are my peace.

Me

Dear You,

I loved you with everything I had only to discover you did not have the capacity for me in your life.

Me

Dear You,

We were beautiful once, before the grey skies
entered...you were the center of my chaos...I found
peace in you...now all I have is pieces of you and
a heart that cries...a piece of me dies each time I
think about where we are now...I don't even know
how we ended up here...we were beautiful once...I
had so much hope...I started to dream again...new
life...new family...a chance to begin again...until it
all blew away...we ran out of words to say...the space
between us got bigger...the skies turned grey...we
were beautiful once...

Me

Dear You,

I kneeled at the base of your tree indulging in fruit that was forbidden to me, touching you was taboo yet your kiss was divine...tracing the curves of your spine... slowly...taking my time...exploring you, discovering you, uncovering you...the tenderness of your skin, the wetness of your lips...the secret between your thighs...the origin of your sighs...the softness of your center...I enjoyed you thoroughly and completely...sharing every inch of me until we both climax continuously...releasing our energies...

Me

Dear You,

You take my thoughts to sacred places...scribbling your name on the walls of my eternity...memories of you flow freely within me...my imagination traces your curves leaving my fingerprints against your secrets...the pleasure of your skin against mine is but a drop in the ocean of intimacy we have created...

Me

Dear You,

The night we shared will not be easily forgotten...
our energies fucked before our bodies every
touched...for most this would be too much but
for us...just enough...a delicate blend between
gentle and rough...somewhere between making
love and hand cuffs...our orgasms danced back
and forth...I enjoyed your naked skin...I found
myself deep within...revealing the secrets of your
universe...with each thrust, I came to know you...
now you are forever a part of me...something
much more than a memory...

Me

Dear You,

I knew by your vocabulary that we would make love beneath many sunsets and sunrises. The wind would whisper your name in times of loneliness. And, our love would ebb and flow, like moon phases on clear starry nights. The words you spoke reveal everything I needed to know about You.

Me

Dear You,

If You were here, or I were there…just know You would be getting thoroughly fucked…sideways.

Me

Dear You,

Given that tomorrow is not promised, I love being your choice today. And, if it's ok with You, I want to spend whatever time we have together holding and loving You.

Me.

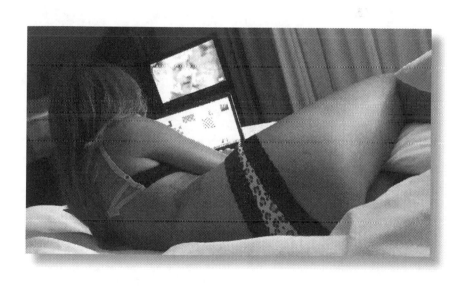

Dear You,

We played across cyberspaces leaving traces of our affection with love notes and smiley faces.

Me

Dear You,

My throb craves the warmth of your wetness.

Me

Dear You,

Damn Netflix…
Let's just fuck and chill.

Me

Dear You,

I spend 90% of my day thinking of new ways to please you.

Me

Dear You,

My need to be naked with You must be satisfied.

Me

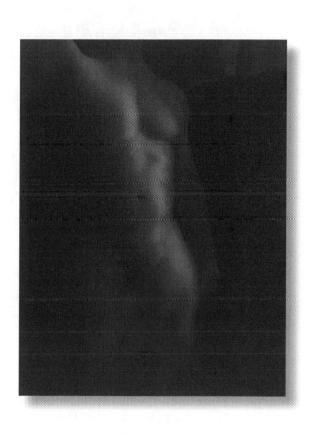

Dear You,

I await You...naked...excited...inviting You to pleasure...craving to swell inside You until I explode.

Me

Dear You,

The taste of You still lingers upon my lips.

Me

Dear You,

We have become the definition of...
Love

Me

Dear You

You flowed past me and your energy reminded me
of memory...past, present, and future collided and
in the midst of that explosion time was reborn as
the universe spun upon the tip of your finger...your
presence still lingers like the kiss from a familiar
stranger not soon forgotten...I still feel you like
I once felt you, intertwined...surrounded by 9's
and 11's...can help but wonder if I ever wander
across the lines that you scribble in the middle of
the night...do you feel these words pulling you
into dizziness...you are unexplained yet I know
you thoroughly...the existence of you makes me
question the existence I once knew...as my soul
gets quiet and I just...feel you.

Me

Dear You,

We defined ourselves "undefined" and by-passed all of the fuckery that most people encounter…no games…no wasted time…no overthinking…just the pure transference of energy of two souls that desired to revolve and evolve around each other…naturally we gravitated toward each other and soon "you and me" became "we" as if we had no other choice but to be together…I loved you before most people decide whether or not to "like" and now I find myself discovering deeper levels of love as I grow even closer to You…

Me

Printed in the United States
By Bookmasters